A Practical Guide to Subtle Brain Injury Claims

Pankaj Madan,
MA (Cantab), Barrister At Law,
Exchange Chambers, Leeds,
Manchester, Liverpool
& 12 King's Bench Walk, Temple, London

Law Brief Publishing

Published 2016 by
Law Brief Publishing
30 The Parks
Minehead
Somerset
TA24 8BT

www.lawbriefpublishing.com

Paperback: 978-1-911035-10-7

PREFACE

I practice in the area of brain injury from mild to very severe catastrophic brain injury (for both Claimants and Defendants). I have focussed in this book upon "Subtle" Brain Injury as it seems to me to be the most difficult and widely misunderstood and under-diagnosed area.

The term "Subtle" brain injury needs to be used cautiously. The term may suggest that the injury is minor when so often the effect may be extremely serious for the individual and the family and may have a very high value in monetary terms.

It is however a convenient term to encompass the sort of brain injury which may for a time, or even indefinitely go untreated or undetected by the medical profession and as a result be uncompensated in the legal process.

I aim here to provide a concise guide to identifying those brain injuries which may otherwise go undetected and uncompensated and aim to provide a short guide to help those bringing and defending such claims.

There are many types of brain injury. I can only here give a brief overview, of "Subtle" Traumatic Brain Injury ("STBI"), what it is, and how to recognise it and what causes it. I will look at whether this is a Psychiatric or Organic injury and whether it is open to abuse by malingerers.

We will then turn to the management of a case involving Subtle Brain Injury and what lawyers can do practically to ensure the best outcome in such a case. Finally we look at one particular decided case.

There is much medicine in this area of the law. I am not a doctor. I have attempted to understand this complex area from experience, medical reports, talking to medical experts, reading medical books and articles. I do not list them here. They are too numerous. I do not mean to be controversial. I try to simplify. By necessity, this can leave out what some may consider to be important. For that I can only apologise.

Finally, I want to make it clear that I have no bias towards Claimants or towards Defendants. Indeed, I act in largely equal measure for both, as members of the Bar usually do.

The aim is only to enlighten this often difficult and underappreciated side of Personal Injury Litigation.

Pankaj Madan
Exchange Chambers & 12 King's Bench Walk
October 2016

Contents

Chapter One	Understanding the Brain	1
Chapter Two	What Can Cause Injury to the Brain?	9
Chapter Three	The Severity of a Traumatic Brain Injury	19
Chapter Four	Neuro-Imaging	25
Chapter Five	The Effects of Traumatic Brain Injury	31
Chapter Six	Why Is Subtle Traumatic Brain Injury Missed?	35
Chapter Seven	Evidence	41
Chapter Eight	The Witness Statement	47
Chapter Nine	Neuropsychological Assessment	57
Chapter Ten	Malingering	65
Chapter Eleven	Surveillance Evidence	71
Chapter Twelve	Damages	77
Chapter Thirteen	Practical Advice	81
Chapter Fourteen	A Case Example: Siegel v Pummel	83
About the Author		87

CHAPTER ONE
UNDERSTANDING THE BRAIN

As an area of medicine, perhaps less than 5% of all there is to be known is in fact, known about the brain, how it operates and how it controls us and how it can deteriorate.

Without this understanding brain injury is one of the most difficult areas of personal injury law.

It increasingly seems to me however that it is also an injury that creates great sadness. Nothing else quite seems to rob the victim and friends and family of the very essence and core of the personality of the person. The body has returned from the accident seemingly sometimes perhaps relatively physically unscathed at least, but the same person often has not.

Diagnosing subtle brain injury is fraught with difficulty not helped by the adversarial process. Damages can be sizeable but damages in themselves are not enough without rehabilitation and structure to a claimant's life.

The human brain is a complex structure with around 100 billion neurons. There are more neurons in the human brain than there are stars that have been observed in the sky.

We need to talk about the structure of the brain. Whilst any doctor or biologist may cringe at the over-simplification of what follows, I apologise, but it is often helpful to simplify rather than complicate.

A neuron also sometimes called a neurone or a nerve cell is the basic building block of the brain. It is a cell not too unlike many other cells in the body but it is electrically excitable and is capable of communicating with other cells through chemical and electrical signals. These occur through "synapses" which are specialised connections.

The neuron is similar to other cells in the body in some ways. It has a "nucleus" which is the core of genetic material making up our cells and a cell membrane. They have similar cell bodies which power the cells and regulate them.

The neuron is made up of the "soma" or cell body and the dendrite and the axon. The dendrite is the tree like extension(s) which extend outward from the cell body increasing the surface area of the cell.

The axon is the elongated fibre which that extends from the cell body. It is often covered in a fatty shielding substance called myelin. Axons then connect with other cells in the body, other neurons, muscle tissue, and organs at junctions called "synapses". The chemicals which cross the synapses are called "neurotransmitters". Electrical signals as well as chemical ones called "action potentials" also communicate information or signals between cells. There are perhaps around 100 identified neurotransmitters, consisting of 6 types. One type are acetylcholines. Amino-acids are another type.

Neurons however are also different to other cells in the body. Crucially, shortly after birth, and in contrast to other types of cell, neurons in most parts of the brain stop reproducing so the adult human has a fixed number of them. The neurons within the hippocampus ,a seahorse shaped structure deep within the brain (responsible for memory amongst other things) and the olfactory bulb (dealing with taste and smell) are exceptions.

Neurons are however able to form new connections with other neurons throughout life. These two facts are important to understand brain injury and rehabilitation. We cannot ever re-generate new brain cells but it is possible to find alternative and new pathways using undamaged brain cells. Neurons possess generally around 1000-10,000 connections to other neurons and 1000 trillion synaptic connections.

Estimates of memory capacity of the human brain if one were to compare it to a computer seem to vary from around 1 Terabyte to 1000 Terabytes of data. There are 1000 Gigabytes in a Terabyte. An average computer hard drive may be around 500GB so best estimates mean that the human brain may store 2000 times the information as the average modern computer.

So, the brain, is complex. It consists of lots of neurons but also structural cells called glial cells and astrocytes which support and protect the neurons As you would expect the brain is also very rich in a network of blood vessels to support and nourish the cells.

The brain is surrounded by the "dura" a thick protective membrane which is next to the skull. There are two further membranes, the Arachnoid which is more loosely attached, and then the Pia Mater which is closely attached to the brain.

It is then held and protected within the skull in a cushion of fluid called the Cerebro-spinal fluid.

The skull is of course extremely hard and unyielding. One ton of pressure is needed to deform and reduce the skull diameter by 1 centimetre. This is what protects the brain from external knocks.

It is this hard unyielding cavity however which can ironically contribute to injury to the brain. It means that the brain if injured internally through sub-dural haematoma has no space to expand. This can result in increased intra-cranial pressure which can injure the deep structures of the brain.

The brain itself can be broadly divided into 3 parts. The 4 sections uppermost towards the skull are together called the "Cerebrum". The Cerebrum controls the "higher" level brain functions.

The 4 parts are called:-

1. The frontal lobe – the area occupying the front half of the skull

2. The Parietal lobe – the area immediately behind the front half of the skull on top of the head;

3. The Occipital lobe – the area at the back of the head above the neck

4. The Temporal lobe – the area at the sides of the brain and extending to behind the ears

The frontal lobe

The frontal lobe controls executive function, decision making skills, personality, language, planning and movement. There is a right and left frontal lobe, one in each of the hemispheres. It is the very essence of "who you are", your personality. The left frontal lobe controls language, verbal skills and positive emotions whilst the right frontal lobe tends to control non-verbal communication and negative emotions. When you are searching for the right word to say, the frontal lobe is responsible. It is also responsible for judgment and attention span regulating mood and emotions. The frontal lobe is also responsible for retaining long term memories which are not task based. Executive based tasks such as planning for the future, organisation and multi-tasking are dealt with by the frontal lobe. The frontal lobe at the point where it rests on the Cribiform plate is particularly vulnerable to diffuse axonal injury. This sort of interference with higher level executive functions and personality changes are a very common complaint following trauma.

If the front part is damaged, any of the following may result:

- Difficulty processing and retaining new information
- Reduced fluency of speech
- Apathy
- Inattentiveness
- Delayed responses to questions
- A lack of inhibition, including socially inappropriate behaviour

If the middle part of the frontal lobe is damaged, people may become apathetic, inattentive and unmotivated. They may describe their thinking as "slowed".

If the middle back part of the frontal lobe is damaged people may have difficulty in expressing themselves in words (expressive aphasia)

The back part of the frontal lobe controls voluntary movement. Weakness or spasticity or paralysis can result from frontal lobe damage. The left side of the lobe controls the right side of the body and the right side of the lobe controls the left side of the body.

The Parietal lobe

The parietal lobe controls intelligence, reasoning, sensation, and our ability to read. Taste, temperature and touch are co-ordinated here. This lobe processes sensory information. Spatial sense is also co-ordinated and processed here. Knowledge of numbers and numeracy is controlled here. The ability to read, interpret words, letters and other symbols is controlled here too. The right hemisphere is more active in left hand dominant people and the left side of the lobe is more active in right hand dominant people.

Damage to the parietal lobe may cause difficulty in recognising or sensing objects by touch. It can cause numbness or impair sensation on one side of the body. People cannot sometimes tell right from left as easily and may have problems sensing where parts of their body are (proprioception).

If the right side of the parietal lobe is damaged people may be unable to do simple tasks such as brushing their hair or dressing themselves. They may have trouble drawing and may get lost in places which should be familiar to them.

The Occipital lobe

The Occipital lobe is largely responsible for vision. It is the main centre for the processing of visual information. If the occipital lobe is damaged on both sides of the brain people may have severely impaired vision or even go blind even though the eyes are physically working fine. This is called cortical blindness. The front part of the lobe controls recognition of familiar objects and people. In some cases vision may become partial. Blocks of visual deficit, (hemaniopia) can occur. As well as direct injury to the back of the head, dissection of a vessel or interruption of the blood supply to this part of the brain in severe frontal or rearward collisions can result in visual deficits.

The Temporal lobe

The Temporal lobe is responsible for language, behaviour, hearing, vision, emotions and memory. The left side of the lobe in most people tends to control language. Damage to the left side of the lobe can therefore result in loss of memory for words and there is often impairment of the ability to understand language.

Areas of the right temporal lobe tend to control recognition of sound and music. This can result in difficulty in singing.

Damage to the temporal lobe can also result in a lack of a sense of humour, obsessiveness, hallucination of bad smells, and they may have a sense of not being able to control their feelings and a sense of "fuzzy" thinking.

Deeper structures

Beneath the Cerebrum is the "Cerebellum" a structure which controls balance, co-ordination and fine muscle control. Damage to this structure may result not so much from direct impact but as a result of raised intra-cranial pressure in response to trauma elsewhere.

Going deeper still, is the "brain stem" which controls the things we do without thinking, such as our heartbeat, breathing and swallowing.

Deeper still at the bottom of the brain, is the spinal cord which extends from the brain all the way to the tail bone. It is about as wide as a small finger.

CHAPTER TWO
WHAT CAN CAUSE INJURY TO THE BRAIN?

Let us get one thing clear first of all. "Head injury" does not mean "brain injury". Head injury can mean injuries not to the brain but injuries to the scalp, skull, face and jaw.

Head injury is therefore an all encompassing term of which brain injury is a sub-set. Brain injury from trauma is normally what Personal Injury lawyers are dealing with and the preferred term is "Traumatic Brain Injury". Where we are dealing with Traumatic Brain Injury which is not at first sight obvious or apparent then the term "SBTI" or subtle traumatic brain injury can be used. It does not imply however that the brain injury is necessarily minor or is not having substantial and very serious effects upon the functioning of the individual.

Injury to the brain can however occur as a result of a number of conditions including:

- Trauma
- Cerebrovascular events
- Degenerative disorders
- Hydrocephalus
- Toxicity
- Infection

- Tumours
- Oxygen deprivation
- Metabolic and endocrine dysfunction
- Nutritional deficiencies

What is a traumatic brain injury?

The first problem is that a head injury and a brain injury are often confused. One can of course sustain an injury to the "head" without sustaining injury to the brain. There may conversely be no visible injury to the "head" yet the brain itself may have sustained an injury.

"Subtle Traumatic Brain injury" or "STBI" is a controversial term. "Undiagnosed" brain injury might be a better term in the first instance.

In the UK there are around 600,000 people seen with head injuries but most of these involve little if any damage to the brain.

Traumatic brain injury is usually considered to be an insult or trauma to the brain as a result of some external force to the brain usually with some diminished or altered state of consciousness. This does not mean that somebody has to be unconscious in order to have demonstrated or suffered a brain injury.

The ICD10 recognises that head injury can be anything from a superficial injury to the head through to an intra-cranial injury. Intra-cranial injury can range from concussion to traumatic amputation of the head.

Traumatic Brain injury ("TBI") is global world health problem and is a major cause of disability. In the UK there are roughly 400 incidents of traumatic head injury per 100,000 of population in any one year and around 240 per 100,000 in the EU as a whole. Overall, males are twice as likely than females to experience a TBI and the risk of traumatic brain injury is particularly high in relation to children. The mortality rate is between 5 and 10 per 100,000 in the UK.

Pie-chart showing the percentage causes of annual TBI related events in the USA

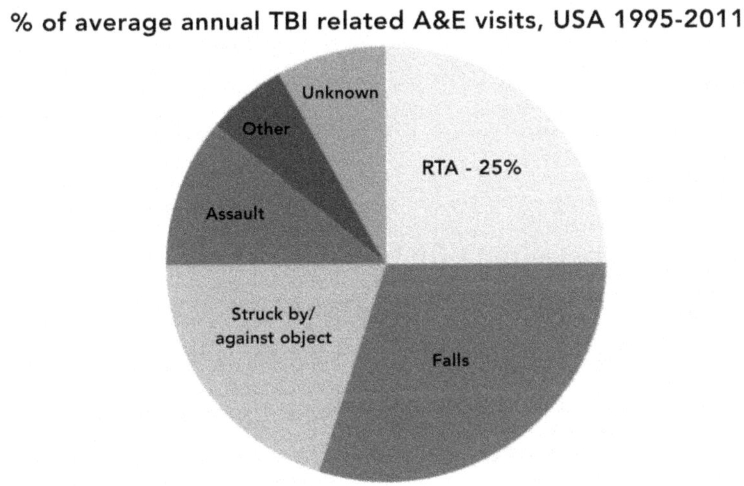

The leading cause of traumatic brain injury is consistently reported as being road traffic accidents, around 21% in the UK and 25% in the USA.

There is some evidence that genetic factors may pre-dispose some people to a poorer outcome following such injury. Some research has shown that the apolipoprotein E has an effect on the deposit of amyloid beta-protein in the cerebral cortex and this is involved in neuro-degeneration. Some people more prone to produce this lipo-protein have been associated with a doubling of likelihood of a poorer outcome at 6 months following a traumatic brain injury.

Types of traumatic brain injury

These may be **closed or blunt** where the dura mater and brain are not penetrated.

Or **open or penetrating** where the dura and brain are penetrated.

Skull fractures or their absence are not always of significance. They do indicate that a substantial amount of force hit the head but of course the area over which the force is distributed may mean that the skull in fact fractures.

Skull fractures may result in CSF leakage however and are an important source of infection and air bubbles. The orbital roof is commonly fractured when for example a person falls backwards hitting the occiput on a hard surface with the shock wave passing through the skull and fracturing the orbital roof which is pretty thin.

Coup and contre-coup

Coup is the expected movement of the brain when for example it decelerates. The rebound movement of the brain, for example rearwards again is the contre-coup.

Heamorrhage which is intra-cranial, inside the skull can be outside the dura or inside the dura. If it is outside or above the dura (see Chapter 1) it is known as an **extradural haemorrhage.** This is as a result of a direct impact to the skull.

If it is beneath the dura it is known as a **sub-dural haemorrhage.**

It is important of course to remember that the force does not have to be applied to the skull in order for a brain injury to occur. The brain is of course for example in a motor vehicle usually moving. When it decelerates suddenly the brain continues to try and move and strikes the inside of the hard skull, the calvarium. Contusions consist of haemorrhage and can carry on bleeding for hours causing a raised intra-cranial pressure. It is a particular problem the older the person gets as the brain atrophies with age and allows for even greater movement within the skull.

Sub-dural haemorrhage which is present soon after the injury is known as acute. If it is only present 1-2 weeks later it is called sub-acute and if it is present more than 2 weeks later it is called chronic sub-dural haemorrhage.

Sub-arachnoid haemorrhage is particularly serious. This often results from an impact to the head and with contusions and lacerations. A laceration around one of the arteries feeding the brain stem often results in immediate collapse and is often fatal

Diffuse Injury

Diffuse Axonal Injury is altogether very different and it is very important in terms of STBI. Diffuse axonal injury can be very serious, even fatal of course and does not necessarily equate with a subtle traumatic brain injury.

Diffuse Axonal Injury ("DAI") is widespread damage to the axons (see Chapter 1 for an explanation about axons) within the brain. Trauma is an accepted cause of DAI as is hypoxia (lack of oxygen to the brain) and hypoglaecemia (lack of nutrition to the cells). DAI caused by trauma is different however, and it can be caused by rapid acceleration or deceleration of the head particularly where there is a rotational movement of the head. This has been accepted by the High Court of England and Wales on numerous occasions as we shall see later.

Traumatic Axonal Injury can cause very severe brain injury resulting in death. In these cases it causes immediate unconsciousness and can result even in persistent vegetative states (PVS). In these severe cases there will be damage to the small blood vessels resulting in spots of blood being present on the MRI scans. These are called "Petechiae" or Petechial haemorrhages.

Damage to the axons results in swollen, torn and damaged fibres in the *white matter* of the brain. Over time, damaged axons may die and there may be shrinkage of the white matter. Ironically therefore, the effects in more minor cases of DAI may take some time to become immediately apparent. Damage to these long fibres can also cause an influx of enzymes and damage to proteins disrupting axonal transport mechanisms and resulting in accumulation of proteins.

The relationship between White matter damage and the effect upon higher executive functions is proving to be very complex to medical science.

Research by Kinnuen, Greenwood and Powell et al. reported in the medical Journal, "Brain" (Brain 2011:134; 449-463) suggests that although chronic and widespread abnormalities of white matter are identifiable following traumatic brain injury, the impact of these changes on cognitive function is likely to depend on the precise damage to key pathways that link nodes in the brain network supporting high level cognitive functions.

The frontal lobe at the point where it rests on the cribiform plate is particularly vulnerable to axonal injury from contrecoup forces following a whiplash type injury mechanism. This is the area which controls executive function and personality.

Diffuse Vascular Injury

In very severe cases of acceleration/deceleration of the brain there can be widespread petechial haemorrhaging. These injuries are generally fatal.

Summary

- Primary brain injury is usually caused by either a direct blow to the head or more usually in our experience of acceleration/deceleration forces on the brain leading to:-
    - Contusional injury (bruising of the brain)
    - Coup (at the site of the impact)
    - Contrecoup (at the opposing side of the impact)

- Diffuse axonal injury (DAI) which is the shearing of axons or fibres connecting neurones or nerve cells together

- Sometimes but not always heamatoma or loss of blood.

There can be DAI without any visible signs on a scan. Many scans are not sensitive to most DAI. CT scans for example are looking for reasonably severe bleeding.

Some forms of advanced MRI scans, T3 MRI for example, can detect more substantial DAI (not usually the torn axons themselves but the associated damage) but even these sensitive scans will still not detect less severe forms of DAI.

- Why not? We must note that axons are much more fragile than even small blood vessels. Even the smallest blood vessels in the brain are much more fibrous, tougher and larger than axons. Where we can pick up some bleeding in the brain therefore even a miniscule amount there is likely to have been diffuse axonal injury.

However, the absence of blood or visible damage on any scan does <u>not</u> mean *the reverse* that there is *no* underlying brain damage in the form of diffuse axonal injury.

Indeed, because the different areas of the brain have different densities in different anatomical areas, injury can result in shearing forces between the areas of different density which can produce major cerebral damage, often with little or nothing to see on the CT or MRI scan. Assessment of the severity or even the existence of such injuries are often difficult both in the short term and the longer term. Rotational forces, such as a side impact therefore where a car spins can have a much more profound effect therefore than first thought.

After primary injury, secondary injury can occur especially in more severe head injury, as a result of Oedema (swelling due to fluid), Hypoxia (lack of oxygen to the nerve cells) and infection.

CHAPTER THREE THE SEVERITY OF A TRAUMATIC BRAIN INJURY

Glasgow Coma Scale

One Scale used to assess consciousness is called the Glasgow Coma Scale which is abbreviated in notes to ("GCS"). This is the most extensively used system for assessing the level of consciousness. The scale is based on the motor (M) verbal (V) and eye-opening (E) responses of the patient and is used to classify injury as "minor", "moderate" or "severe". The scale does not go to 0. The minimum score representing complete unconsciousness is 3. Traditional thinking is as follows:-

13-15 means you may be likely to be dealing with a **Mild or Minor** injury

9-12 means you may be likely to be dealing with a **Moderate** injury

Less than or equal to 8 usually means a **severe** injury

Note that 15/15 on the GCS scale means fully conscious. Nevertheless, subtle traumatic brain injury is still possible even where ambulance notes or especially the A&E notes document a GCS of 15/15. These scores are often recorded many minutes after an accident has occurred.

Other factors can also affect the level of consciousness such as alcohol or the administration of sedating drugs such as some pain relieving medication (although usually only by 1 or 2 points).

Equally, sometimes these factors are assumed to be the cause of impaired consciousness when in fact the cause may well be a brain injury.

A GCS score of 3, the lowest score, represents no eye opening to pain, no verbal response and no motor response to pain. This would be recorded in the notes as E1, V1, M1.

A fully conscious score of 15 would be recorded as E4, V5, M6.

It is not just the total score that matters. Claimants with the same total score but differing components of the scores can have different outcomes.

It is easily forgotten that there may be other signs of brain injury and in the medico-legal context there can be an over-emphasis of the importance of GCS scores.

Signs of injury on the scalp such as bruising and lacerations, depressed skull fractures, sub-conjunctival haemorrhages bleeding, and discharge of CSF from the ear or nose may be indicators of brain injury. The latter are particularly associated with skull base fractures. Anosmia or loss of the sense of smell may also be an indicator of brain injury.

It is also wrong to assume that any fall in the level of consciousness with time cannot be due to brain injury. It may be falsely associated with medical treatment. In fact, raised intra-cranial pressure may also cause a decrease in the level of consciousness over time in the aftermath of the hours after the traumatic event. The cranium is of course a rigid box containing the brain. Any increase in volume caused by blood, swelling of the brain or CSF can cause raised intra-cranial pressure and a fall in the level of consciousness. If left untreated, death may soon occur.

Such victims of brain injury are the "walking wounded". Seemingly normal at first but with a fatal outcome. This is why of course CT scanning in the accident and emergency context is extremely useful. It is being used to detect and exclude the possibility of a bleed leading to raised intra-cranial pressure and the possibility of a severe outcome or death.

The Mayo system

The Mayo system is a different classification system of brain injury.

It was developed to deal with some of the difficulties arising from the use of GCS to identify a Mild Traumatic Brain Injury. The Mayo system has several main categories:-

1. Definite moderate-severe traumatic Brain Injury;
2. Probable moderate traumatic brain injury
3. Possible Traumatic Brain Injury

The scale utilises multiple criteria including loss of consciousness, post-traumatic amnesia, skull fracture and evidence of neuro-radiological abnormalities. To fall into the moderate severe category there would usually have to be loss of consciousness of 30 minutes or more and Post traumatic amnesia of more than 24 hours.

The Mayo system is generally thought of as far more reliable than GCS scale score at identifying brain injury and the severity of it.

Post-traumatic amnesia is a very important component of identifying whether or not there has been a brain injury and the severity of it.

Post-traumatic amnesia is the interval from injury until the patient can form and lay down and recall new memories.

One research paper by Nakase-Richardson et al (2011) concluded that:-

- a PTA of 0-14 days was classified as a moderate TBI,
- a PTA of 15-28 days was classified as a moderately severe TBI,
- and a PTA of 29-70 days or more was classified as a severe TBI.

Other factors are also taken into account including the presence of dizziness and nausea and headache.

The Mayo system of classification is multi-factorial and has been shown to be sensitive with a high degree of reliability on predicting brain injury and the outcome of it.

One problem however particularly in the in the UK is that there is usually no prospective tool used for the assessment of post-traumatic amnesia in the clinical setting. Assessments of PTA are therefore being made retrospectively. Friedland, writing in an article in "Spine" 2013, S4, states that the retrospective analysis of post-traumatic amnesia can yield false positives in terms of diagnosing and individual as suffering from a TBI

The "Russell" System of Classification of brain injury

The Russell system depends heavily on the level of Post traumatic amnesia and injuries are classified as follows:-

- Mild – PTA of less than 1 hour
- Moderate – PTA of more than 1 hour but not more than 24 hours
- Severe – PTA or more than 24 hours but not more than 1 week
- Very severe – PTA of more than 1 week but less than 1 month
- Extremely severe – PTA of more than 1 month

It is difficult in a *legal* book of this size to give a comprehensive analysis. A brief summary however is as follows:- A TBI is moderate to severe if one or more features exist:-

- Loss of consciousness of 30 minutes or more
- Post traumatic amnesia of 24 hours or more
- The lowest GCS score in the first 24 hours is 12 or less
- Haemorrhagic contusion, Penetrating TBI, Sub-arachnoid haemorrhage, brain stem injury, intra-cerebral heamatoma, sub-dural heamatoma or any of them are present.
- The length of post traumatic amnesia (the length of time before continuous memory is re-established) is one of the better indicators of traumatic brain injury.
- Abnormalities on neuro-imaging will influence the conclusion.

Mild to moderate TBI may be diagnosed if there is :

- Loss of consciousness of less than 30 minutes
- Post traumatic amnesia of less than 24 hours
- Depressed, basilar or linear skull fracture without penetration of the dura mater

A diagnosis of symptomatic possible TBI may be made if one or more of the following signs are present:-

- Blurred vision, confusion, dizziness, headache or nausea and/or vomiting.

It is worth remembering however that there is no "gold standard" in relation to classification systems for brain injury. It is important that they are understood and the various limitations of each appreciated.

CHAPTER FOUR
NEURO-IMAGING

Imaging in the accident and emergency department is generally performed if there is suspicion of a brain injury or there are substantial neurological deficits. Acute imaging is aimed at identifying problems which need urgent surgical intervention or medical attention to alleviate further injury or death.

The most available form of useful scan is therefore the Computed Tomography or "CT" scan and it is the result of this which is most normally available in the Claimant's medical notes. CT scans impose very high radiation doses often equivalent to 500 x-rays at once. Clinical and investigatory use has to be justified.

It has largely replaced the use of skull x-rays as it is quick and available and detailed. It identifies quickly bleeds, clotted or otherwise which require stemming or removal of clots.

If the GCS has dropped below 13 at any time since injury or is still at 13 or 14 at 2 hours post injury then the NICE guidelines suggest that scanning should be carried out. There are other elements to the criteria as well and the full criteria can be found at www.nice.org.uk.

Imaging after the acute phase

Magnetic Resonance Imaging or "MRI" is the imaging of choice however to reveal brain injuries. MRI does not involve any significant radiation dose. It is not used in the acute phase because it is impractical and often not available but it can be used afterwards to obtain a clearer picture of the extent of injury and in particular is much more useful in being able to detect Diffuse Axonal Injury caused by those shearing or acceleration-deceleration forces.

DAI is usually seen in the White matter, the corpus callosum and the pontine-mesencaephalic junction. It is often seen at the borders of the grey cortical matter and the white matter due to the different physical properties of the grey and white matter resulting in the shearing of tissue at these points under deceleration-acceleration forces particularly rotational forces.

The imaging of choice is now 3T MRI examination of the brain with gradient echo and SWI (susceptibility weighted imaging) which assesses the extent of micro-bleeds and residual brain damage. The T stands for Tesla. 3T is twice as sensitive as 1.5 T MRI in detecting diffuse axonal injury.

3T MRI with SWI is the most sensitive technique available in clinical practice to detect evidence of micro-haemorrhage. These are low signal intensity lesions which occur due to the deposit of a substance called "haemosiderin". This substance has a high magnetic susceptibility so therefore shows up even in small amounts.

This is particularly important in assessing traumatic brain injury. If there have been micro-haemorrhages, because the small vessels are tougher and more fibrous and larger than the axons, the disruption of the vessels causing micro bleeds is a pretty sure sign that there will have been disruption of the axons as well. In other words it is a marker of the trauma that the axons will have been subjected to at that point in the brain.

In summary, MRI scanning, especially 3T may be useful but will not always detect the micro-haemorrhaging associated with subtle traumatic brain injury. The actual individual axons themselves cannot be imaged. Diffuse axonal injury can occur without the associated bleeding as we have discussed.

A good Neuro-radiologist however could bring tremendous knowledge to a case often being able to pinpoint the site of a brain injury which had hitherto gone undetected or where the claim was suspected to be psychological or malingering. If the site of injury detected accords with the sort of symptoms one would expect from the damage to that area of the brain the Claimant's case is often unassailable.

Conversely, the lack of detectable damage does not necessarily mean there is no brain injury due to the limitations in scanning techniques.

SPECT maybe useful. This is Single photon computed tomography. This is nuclear medicine imaging technique for the evaluation of blood-flow. A radio-nucleotide is bound to a compound that crosses the blood brain barrier and is trapped for at least the length of time required to image the patient.

Diffusion weighted imaging (DWI) and diffusion tensor imaging (DTI) may be useful. This relies on the difference between isotropic diffusion of water molecules in a normal and injured brain.

PET, Positron Emission Tomography measures the accumulation of positron emitting radioisotopes within the brain.

3T MRI scanning is likely to be the most helpful and is probably the imaging of choice as discussed before. It is conducted at some London clinics in the UK and as of the date of writing there is also a T3 MRI scanning machine in Newcastle-Upon-Tyne

White matter disruption is an important determinant of cognitive impairment after brain injury and the location of the disruption can lead a good neuro-radiologist to predict the cognitive functions likely to be impaired such as memory and higher executive functions.

There are knock on effects of course. Once there has been micro-bleeding in the brain tissue, adjacent cells also may be damaged.

The field of neuro-radiology is rapidly changing and new techniques are evolving all the time to provide more information about the extent of injury, underlying physiological changes and anatomy.

Summary

- the absence of brain injury on a CT scan is in no way determinative that there has been no traumatic brain injury;
- Post-acute imaging *may* reveal the presence of injury possibly in the form of Diffuse Axonal Injury, the hallmark of which is micro-haemorrhaging
- Micro-haemorrhaging is strongly associated with subsequent cognitive deficits particularly affecting executive function.
- The absence of micro-heamorrhage however even on the most sensitive scans does not mean that there is no diffuse axonal injury. This is because axons are more fragile than the tougher, lar-

ger more fibrous vessels so there can be diffuse axonal injury even without signs on the scan.

CHAPTER FIVE
THE EFFECTS OF TRAUMATIC BRAIN INJURY

It is important to remember that most mild TBI patients make a good recovery, generally 95%. Post-concussional syndrome (PCS) is a label or diagnosis given to the many who do not. It is sometimes especially by neurosurgeons regarded as a somatoform disorder and is treated by way of Cognitive Behavioural Therapy and anti-depressant medication.

Sometimes however persisting impairments are more probable and may lead to reduced mental speed, attention mental inefficiency, fuzzy thinking, difficulty process complex information or tasks with multiple elements, fatigue and irritability.

The functions of the different areas of the brain

The left side

The left side of the brain deals with language, movement of the right side of the body, verbal and analytical thinking, encoding of verbal information, semantic memory (knowledge and information), deductive reasoning and verbal memory.

The right side

In most people, the right side deals with some degree of language if left handed, movement of the left side of the body, visual and spatial reasoning, retrieval of information, episodic information, inductive reasoning and visual memory.

The frontal lobes and executive function

The terms frontal lobe syndrome and "dysexecutive syndrome" and organic personality disorder are often used loosely.

Executive functions are concerned with recognising that something needs to be done and with planning and initiating and regulating such behaviour.

The orbito-frontal region

This is involved with behavioural control and insight and problems include a lack of insight, impulsive behaviour, irrational behaviour, disinhibition, poor temper control, obsessive behaviour and egocentricity

The dorso-lateral region

This is involved in cognitive problems that may include mental juggling, inefficient recall of information, reduced fluency, concrete, rigid or inflexible thinking, reduced ability to estimate.

The medial region

Damage to this region may result in problems such as a lack of drive, lack of initiative, apathy, flatting or absence of emotion.

These problems occur often in combination and with varying degrees of severity.

Effects of Head injury

Broadly there are 3 consequences to head injury:

1. Physical consequences

2. Cognitive consequences

3. Emotional Consequences

Physical consequences

The physical consequences are often clear such as the loss of sight, headaches, and other obvious physical signs.

Cognitive consequences

Cognitive abilities comprise memory thinking and communicating. The most common problems are memory problems. Memory events which happen well before the injury are not usually impaired unless the injury was extremely severe and memory events which happen well before the injury are usually not badly impaired. What is common is difficulty in learning new information, retraining, and retrieving such information.

The speed with which they approach any task including cognitive tasks are therefore slower. Keeping track of more than one thing at a time. They may become overloaded and frustrated. Problems in language and communication can also be common. Forgetting names even those they could not reasonably expect to forget can occur. Concrete thinking is also common. These problems occur from damage to the frontal part of the brain. These frontal deficits can be very subtle, not evident to the casual observer and sometimes even cognitive testing does not uncover them.

Emotional consequences

Changes in emotion and behaviour are very common after more severe head injury. Very early after injury, while the patient is still confused, abusive and uncontrolled behaviour is common.

CHAPTER SIX
WHY IS SUBTLE TRAUMATIC BRAIN INJURY MISSED?

Unless there is an open head wound, or long lasting unconsciousness or drowsiness the head injury is not likely to be the focus of initial medical attention particularly where there are also gross orthopaedic injuries and soft tissue injuries which require urgent attention.

This focus on the most initially debilitating injuries continues into the Personal Injury claim with experts being obtained solely to report upon such obvious physical injuries. Early conferences in person are often not held due to financial pressures on cost and distances which are now omni-present between lawyers and their clients.

Family and the Claimant will often put such subtle changes initially down to the shock of the accident and changed circumstances.

Secondly, initial loss of consciousness lasting maybe only minutes will not usually be apparent to the ambulance services and the Accident and Emergency Departments. It is common for the ambulance services to take 10 to 20 minutes after an accident to arrive at the scene. Any witness to the unconsciousness often does not make a statement (although there may be one in a police report). The statement may not deal with the unconsciousness anyway. If liability however is not in dispute, often the police report is never obtained. Sometimes, lawyers may also not obtain or peruse carefully the ambulance reports. Reports of drowsiness and GCS score ratings may be overlooked. Furthermore, normal GCS scores may be recorded because of the length of time elapsed since the accident.

Thirdly, there is often a lack of insight into any subtle head injury by the Claimant. Changes are often not recognised or admitted by the victim themselves and it is often only at a detailed conference with the claimant and members of his family or his or her spouse that the details of the head injury are revealed. This can worryingly be many years after lawyers have been dealing with the claim. Undoubtedly, many subtle brain injuries are missed.

Fourthly, there is a difficulty even amongst doctors, whether treating or medico-legal, in recognising and diagnosing subtle or mild traumatic brain injury. There are many who feel that a lack of a reduced GCS score at A & E for example suggests a lack of any brain injury even though this may be many minutes or even hours after the accident occurred.

Fifthly, there is a focus upon Glasgow Coma Scale Score or unconsciousness as an indicator of brain injury. We have already discussed the alternative systems of classification more appropriate to more subtle forms of brain injury. There is no prospective tool used in the NHS acute clinical setting for the assessment of post-traumatic amnesia and scanning of the brain is at most usually limited to a CT scan looking for gross bleeding.

For these reasons, subtle brain injury is perhaps not infrequently missed.

What signs should lawyers be looking for?

1. **The accident** – Firstly, the mechanism and type of accident should give us a clue. We are looking for accidents where there is likely to have been some substantial acceleration or deceleration forces acting on the brain itself. Such accidents are likely to be high velocity side on collisions, motorbike or bike accidents, high velocity frontal collisions, pedestrian accidents and falls from height. Substantial road traffic accidents particularly causing a rotational element to the head should not be dismissed however as we will see.

2. **A reduced GCS score** – either in the Ambulance notes or the A&E notes themselves. The ambulance notes may form part of the A&E notes. If they are missing you can and should contact the Ambulance Service that attended.

3. **Reports of "head injury" or "concussion"** – Other medical reports such as from Orthopaedic Surgeons may mention in passing concussion or head injury. Sometimes, they often do not make much of such symptoms or investigate them or make appropriate recommendations.

4. **History from the Claimant or Claimant's family** – it often starts with a complaint that the Claimant is now "different" and "not the person that she was". If you don't listen out for it you may dismiss it. If however you ask, "tell me more about that" or "how so?" you often start to hear some of the following symptoms:-

- Pre and/or Post-Traumatic Amnesia – This is still one of the best indicators of brain injury if a careful history is taken and a careful analysis of the notes is undertaken. Further details are within the chapter on witness statements and in relation to the Mayo Classification System. PTA is the inability to lay down clear and continuous memories. To have PTA the Claimant does not need to still have been unconscious;

- Loss of control – The Claimant has a short fuse, rapid mood swings, occasionally violence. It may be an exaggeration of a pre-injury behaviour trait;

- Apathy – The Claimant may appear depressed but denies it. The Claimant lacks the drive to do anything and often gets up late. This often results from damage to the frontal lobes;

- Extreme tiredness – The Claimant often wakes late and has difficulty in staying awake. If they work, they will often go to bed as soon as they get home and have difficulty in getting up in the morning. When tired the victim may slur speech and appear drunk or on drugs. Often with young victims parents may actually suspect drug abuse but testing is negative. Difficulty in staying awake can result from damage to the brain stem;

- Depressed mood – Around 2/3rds of people will feel depressed during the first 5 years of injury. It doesn't diminish and often gets worse. It is often really "low mood" rather than true depression;

- Tension and anxiety – around 2/3rds feel tense and anxious. It doesn't diminish with treatment;

- Alcohol intolerance – this is rarely asked about but in many cases, I have found that the Claimant when prompted in neutral terms about how they like or enjoy a drink come out with the fact that they can no longer "hold" their alcohol anymore. Even 1 pint of beer seems to cause them to have slurred speech or makes them unstable or exacerbates embarrassing or rude behaviour- disinhibition. It's difficult to see how this will usually be a psychological symptom;

- Difficulty in doing more than one thing at once (multi-tasking);

- Impaired sense of taste or smell;

- Word finding or retrieval difficulties;

- Poor memory, attention or concentration – many complain about poor memory. Forgetting familiar things such as the names of people that they know well, routes that they would have known. They find that they are having to make lists and frequently forget things. There is often huge reliance on a spouse or family member to help them structure the day. Mobile telephone bills often tell the story with many calls per day between the brain injured victim and their helper. Some have difficulty in concentrating on a TV programme or book;

- Headaches – This is a common complaint and is a cause for concern especially where they are continuing many months or even years after the accident and where they are no longer associated with a whiplash type injury to the neck. Such pain is also often localised;

- Visual disturbances and tinnitus – These are perhaps less commonly reported but can be a consequence of traumatic brain injury. Dizziness and vertigo sometimes are also a consequence.

The best history is usually given by a member of the family. It is very important therefore where brain injury is suspected firstly not to suggest it to the victim or the family but to allow the history to come out through non-leading, probing type questions. If in any doubt, perhaps have an early conference with specialist counsel.

What do you do if you suspect brain injury?

You will obviously need to tell the Claimant that there is a possibility they have sustained a closed STBI and that you need further evidence to investigate this. It is important not to be suggestive. I often say we are doing this as a precaution to "rule it out". The suggestion of Iaterogeneis or the legal claim creating the suggestion of a brain injury may rightly be made by Defendants in appropriate cases.

CHAPTER SEVEN
EVIDENCE

We turn then to the evidence that will be reasonably required to resolve the proceedings. We must remember that the case is likely to be subject to a costs budget. The District Judge or Master will have to be satisfied that the expert evidence obtained is

a) Reasonably required to resolve the proceedings;

b) To be obtained on a unilateral rather than joint basis;

c) Is proportionate in cost to the value in dispute, importance and complexity of the proceedings.

Necessity is trumped by proportionality and before embarking on expensive evidence we need to consider budgets, the overall value of the claim and proportionality. The evidence required is likely to be all or some of the disciplines as follows:

- A Neuropsychologist
- A Neurosurgeon or Neurologist, (probably the latter) and not usually both;
- A Neuro-radiologist
- A Neuropsychiatrist
- Possibly, a Consultant in Neuro-rehabilitation Medicine (although not always).

If you are a claimant's lawyer you may wish to remember that neurologists vary in their knowledge and acceptance of STBI largely because they only see or treat the more severe forms of injury placing perhaps great reliance on GCS scores and visible bleeding.

I had a recent conference with a Professor of Neurosurgery who assured me that persisting symptoms due to brain injury in the form of Diffuse Axonal Injury was just not possible in the claimant's case. It was a serious case involving a severe fall from height with unconsciousness, but the expert said that the question of serious persisting brain injury didn't arise because the loss of consciousness did not to him seem long enough.

I was reasonably convinced that he was wrong and I took him to the case Law on the subject and we discussed the Mayo Criteria and what the High Court Judge, Mr Justice Wilkie had found in relation to Diffuse Axonal Injury in the case of Siegel v Pummel 2014. He read the detailed 100 page judgment and emailed me and our Solicitor a few days later. He had meanwhile now looked more closely at the medical literature and sent it to us.

He told us that he had not really been aware of this before and that the Claimant's symptoms were probably of diffuse axonal injury. The mechanism of the accident was probably entirely consistent with the brain damage and symptoms being elicited by the Claimant. He was less concerned now about loss of consciousness but the overall levels of pre and post-traumatic amnesia and thought this the better indicator of the severity of the brain injury. He was also persuaded by the neuropsychological evidence which he had now seen.

It may take the detailed analysis of a neuropsychologist to elicit the diagnosis of a STBI.

Even then, the diagnosis is fraught with difficulty. Indeed, for this reason it is sometimes better to *start* with *Disclosure* and then follow on from that, that is to say:-

1. Notes – obtain the medical notes and ambulance notes.

2. Witness statements – progress onto the witness statements from the claimant and immediate family;

3. Treatment – now progress onto psychological treatment by an experienced local (Neuro) psychologist and see what their view and findings are. Do they feel that the Claimant is brain injured or are the findings consistent only with a psychological condition.

Treatment under the NHS is often very much rationed on the grounds of resources even if the preliminary acute treatment path did identify a brain injury.

4. Neuropsychologist – Then, obtain the treatment notes and a report from the treating expert and only then go onto perform testing with a formal report from a Part 35 instructed Neuropsychologist *before* instructing the Neurologist.

5. Neuro-Radiologist – At all times consider whether any further radiology in the form of T3 MRI scanning in particular is needed now (as a medico-legal report) or whether that should await confirmation of need from the Neurologist. It is im-

possible to say when or what scan as all cases differ. Seek the advice of a neuro-radiologist.

6. Neurologist – Then instruct your neurologist. The Neurologist has a much better set of tools and evidence with which to assess the severity and duration of any brain injury.

7. Consider the need for other experts – Neuro-psychiatrist and Consultant in Neuro-Rehabilitation Medicine.

It also very useful to try and treat any psychological overlay or symptoms first before proceeding to neuropsychological testing as failure of effort can be due to severe psychological symptoms rather than malingering.

This method gives the Neurologist and Neuropsychiatrist another tool with which to opine whether the Claimant has a persisting brain injury or not and to gauge the severity of it. Most importantly the Claimant is receiving treatment from an early stage thus providing the best possible prognosis. Early treatment is best. The best evidence is that any recovery from an organic brain injury occurs during the first 36 months after trauma.

The detailed perfected witness statement should also be provided to the expert who can use it as evidence just as the Court will at trial. It makes the assessment process easier for the Claimant and for the expert.

This may be the reverse of the way in which Solicitors are used to dealing with cases.

Many would instruct the expert first, indeed often before disclosure of medical notes is even complete, with no witness statement. That is not always wrong but if it is done, it should probably be a preliminary or draft report at this stage or even just result in oral advice in conference.

The witness statement is then done only when ordered by the Court. This omits the importance of the witness statement particularly with a brain injured claimant who may find it harder to remember and structure their thoughts in interview with the medical expert. Accurate analysis of PTA is very important.

If you haven't done this, the best neurologists should know this however and will set aside a sufficient length of time for an interview and will be careful to ascertain as precisely as possible the levels and timescale of and for pre-traumatic and post-traumatic amnesia which can often be the one of the best indicators of brain injury.

If you are representing a Defendant you will certainly wish also to obtain your own evidence and to choose a neurologist and neuro-psychologist and (Neuro)-Psychiatrist with some care. Instruct early too. Don't wait until post issue.

Ask to see the treatment notes and consider some well-placed interim payments which even if causation is in dispute may be of considerable benefit in the long run.

If you are going to use specialist Counsel, instruct early with the complete set of notes and then have a detailed conference with Counsel first and then also with your Counsel and experts to discuss causation and diagnosis and your plan. Are you going to offer treatment or will it simply be counter-productive for this particular Claimant? Is the Defendant going to accept that there is a brain injury here or is diagnosis and causation going to be heavily disputed.

CHAPTER EIGHT
THE WITNESS STATEMENT

Memories fade with the passage of time. Not all memory is the same however. Traumatic events such as an accident are normally strong memories which we retain. Indeed one of the problems which may arise is Post-traumatic stress disorder where the memories are so powerful they cannot be properly processed and properly placed into the long term memory. Victims re-experience the accident as if they were reliving it in the form of nightmares and intrusive thoughts which have a deleterious effect upon health.

Memory can be episodic and semantic. Semantic memories are generally for facts and dates.

Episodic memories is like the film running in our head which records events and then puts them in the appropriate place, more usually placing the events in the "recycling bin" which is then emptied once long enough has passed.

Episodic memories in cases of true post traumatic amnesia cannot be recalled by the person even when give a "cue".

This is why an early, clear and precise witness statement is so important in subtle traumatic brain injury cases. This is also why it is essential to distinguish between what the Claimant has been told about the accident and its aftermath and what the Claimant can actually recall.

It is an essential tool to actually evaluate the brain injury itself and a powerful piece of evidence for the experts and the Judge.

Other evidence from witnesses to the accident are also very important to be able to help establish what events actually occurred, the levels of consciousness of the Claimant after the accident and what events occurred in the aftermath or indeed before the accident which the claimant is unable to remember.

It is also vital that the Claimant is not led, prompted or encouraged to say that he does or doesn't remember something. Therefore open, non-leading questions should be asked. These usually begin with the letter "W". I call it "the rule of W". Questions such as "what, where, when, and why" (also perhaps "How"?) are usually non-leading questions. As soon as the questioner starts saying things like "is it" or "could it be that"- then you are probably leading.

A leading question is one which suggests the desired answer and is most effectively used in cross-examination of witnesses adverse to your case. If you are cross examining the brain injured Claimant to prove your theory of a brain injury you are doing him or her a disservice and setting your firm up for a fall.

Good clinicians, and Counsel should always be careful to elicit non-leading questions particularly important in brain injury cases. Medico-legal appointments with experts, lasting only 20 minutes or half an hour in this context may well have been conducted badly.

It is vital also to tell the claimant the difference at the outset between having been told or gleaned something by what other people have said and their own actual recall. The question is always what can they recall not what do they know.

The expert witnesses too must be very careful in their analysis of eliciting the claimant's evidence. I believe that a witness statement taken carefully at an early stage can be the critical difference between a successful and a weak case at trial.

All the usual rules in relation to witness statements and those which can be found in part 32 of the Civil Procedure Rules of course still apply. All witness statements should be in the witnesses own words but this really must be observed precisely and fully with a brain injured claimant.

First you need to speak to the family or partner who accompanies the claimant and obtain the background facts and the events they know. This gives benchmark for the events that have happened which the claimant may not remember.

It will also be helpful to have the ambulance and A & E notes and the hospital notes if applicable and all well ordered and legible.

Then take your witness statement from the claimant in the early stages. Don't let family or a partner interrupt even though they should be present and make this clear at the outset as to the reasons why so you don't appear to be rude.

Then go on to take the witness statement from the partner or family who accompanies. This may need to be done over the course of a day or on separate occasions. You need to cater for the fact that the Claimant may well become much more fatigued than any other client.

Observe quietly, word finding difficulties, slurred speech, losing track and the train of thought. Consider (with consent) unobtrusively recording the interview so you can go back to it when you are typing up the witness statement and keep it is as record in case of suggestion of legal Iaterogenesis to prove the open ended nature of the questioning.

Don't dismiss witness evidence of people outside the circle of close family and friends who will also have observed over time the differences in the claimant. A good example may be somebody the claimant spends time with on a frequent basis even if it is not lengthy.

The obvious examples are the barber or hairdresser, long standing- GP, local shop-keepers, work colleagues, even customers. Make sure they can provide examples otherwise they are likely to be undermined. Don't call too many witnesses.

Remember they Court's power to limit witnesses and think of the time and costs. Just use the best witnesses, not all of them.

The Structure of the Claimant's Witness statement

The following structure should probably be adopted although it is not an inflexible rule.

1. Pre-Accident

- State of health
- Educational Achievements
- Employment history
- Events of the day before the accident

- Previous accidents and injuries

2. The Accident

- What if anything is remembered about the accident
- What they have learned since and from who and how
- Evidence of experience or practice or for example about the motorbike or their riding experience, wearing a helmet, lights etc.
- Post traumatic amnesia – when did continuous memory return. The Claimant can have islands or pockets of memory without the return of continuous memory
- A past care history provided by family is essential for the care expert.

3. Description of Post accident problems

3(a). Physical problems

- Mobility
- Limb movement- weaknesses, tremors, spasms, proprioception (knowing where the limb is oriented)
- Continence of bowel and bladder;
- Skin Care
- Balance, dizziness, co-ordination

- Double vision, Visual Acuity, Double vision. Blocking out of visual fields known as "Hemaniopia"
- Hearing/tinnitus/Hyperacusis/Headaches
- Facial appearance, body appearance- weight gain
- Speech or word finding problems
- Epilepsy, absences, depression, mental health issues.
- Impaired sense of taste and smell, changed eating habits
- Fatigue, poor sleep habits and increased awakening;
- Abnormal sensations of temperature or feeling unduly cold or warm;

3(b). Cognitive problems

- Intellectual impairments
- Visual problems e.g. processing
- Verbal problems, word finding, expression of speech,
- Memory- problems in processing information, words, faces, numbers, immediately and retaining the information, working memory, speed of information processing, keeping attention and being distracted. Difficulty in being able to think or do more than one task at the same time.

- Ability to concentrate on one job. Is the claimant able to read books, newspapers or magazines in the same way. Does he watch soaps or films and can he or she understand the plot (at least as well as they always could before the accident)
- Do they have insight into their problems or is it just other people who say there is a problem?
- Do they misinterpret words or other people's behaviour. Are they better one to one than in a crowd?
- Organisation and planning, ability to think ahead as to the consequences of the claimant's action or inaction;
- Ability to budget and manage finances;
- Speech and language problems
- Poor judgement.

3(c). Behavioural and Emotional Problems

- Changed personality
- Anxiety
- Mood swings
- Anger or aggression and effect on relationships
- Egocentricity

- Repetitive behaviour
- Disinhibition
- Problems with motivation and initiation
- Depression, suicide and paranoia. Substance abuse

3(d). Capacity

- Does the claimant understand the information given
- Can he retain the information given
- Can he weigh up the retained information to use it in the decision making process;
- Can he make the decision and communicate it;
- Can examples be given where he has failed in understanding information;
- Can anything be overcome by the use of aids, written information, pictures, speaking to the Claimant when well rested and in short bursts and with written notes.

Summary

- Obtain an early witness statement from the Claimant;

- It must be obtained in a non-leading way and deal with the levels of PTA;
- It is a difficult skill to take this statement. Don't leave it to the most junior person in the firm. Consider the early use of specialist counsel;
- Structure and detail matters!;
- Witness statements should always be in his or her own words. Particular care needs to be taken with the Claimant;
- Take witness statements from the family but don't ignore those further away from the claimant who see him or her on a regular basis;
- The witness evidence is often the difference between success and failure in such cases. Both sides can produce expert evidence. Careful witness evidence is rather more difficult to come by.

CHAPTER NINE
NEUROPSYCHOLOGICAL ASSESSMENT

Neuropsychology is that branch of psychology which specialises in the assessment of patients with focal brain injury or neurocognitive deficits. Neuropsychologists study and report upon how brain structure and function relate to specific psychological processes.

The neuropsychological approach uses tests designed to reflect specifically different aspects of cognitive function. Poor performance may indicate focal or localised brain damage. Poor performance on a series of tests may reflect diffuse axonal injury or a mixture of the two of course.

The purposes of testing is as follows:-

1. To give a neurocognitive profile of a person – for example whether they are or were High IQ individuals before the accident;

2. Repeated testing over time (not usually within 6-9 months) can give an insight into changes in cognitive functioning and any improvements or indeed deterioration;

It is important to note that the tests in themselves do not conclusively, diagnose brain injury. No set of tests can provide a complete map of brain function. They can give an indication of the underlying problem.

Furthermore, an apparently normal performance on psychological tests should be interpreted cautiously. As individuals recover from brain damage they often utilise alternative strategies to overcome the remaining deficits

Tests are reasonably objective and are standardised so that the Claimant can be compared with "normal" individuals and "brain injured individuals".

Statements can be made about the probability of the result being correct.

Results may help to establish whether there has been a brain injury and if the extent of cognitive and executive impairments. Mental capacity to deal with the litigation can also be established.

Neuropsychological testing will also assess current intellectual abilities including:

- Verbal skills
- Non-Verbal skills
- Working memory – Working memory is a form of short term memory which allows somebody to hold and play with information for a short amount of time. For example, when you look up a name or number and then hold it in your memory for just enough time to write it down.
- Processing speed
- Memory through verbal and visual learning, recall and recognition

- Executive skills such as planning, problem solving, judging and estimating, fluency and dividing and selective switching of attention.

In a typical neuropsychological assessment there are a series or battery of tests. Here are the most commonly used:-

Tests of Cognitive performance validity

1. **The Reliable Digit Span Test** – This is a test of working memory. The individual is presented with a long series of numbers and then the same thing in reverse. This tests the ability to manipulate information and deal with sequencing. Then the ability to test how many times they can consistently do this in a row is tested. There are unusual patterns if faking a brain injury so there are validity scores as well.

2. **The Conners' Continuous Performance Test** – This also tests working memory but it is not as sensitive as the above test. The tests are a measure of the ability to maintain concentration over a period of time. One of the common coping strategies of brain injury victims is that they slow down. Being excessively slow is what people who are faking may do. The neuropsychologist measures how many targets they keep missing. Problems in sustaining concentration lead to erratic results. It is uncommon to miss targets or to be extreme in their reaction times. There are cut off scores used to identify those who are not putting in full effort.

3. **The Advanced Clinical Solutions Effort Test** – This continually assesses effort. It uses normative data and compares people's performance relative to the normal population and to those known to be suffering from brain injury. These tests are easy even for those with brain injury.

4. **The Wisconsin Card Sorting Test** – This is a test which is sensitive to brain damage and frontal lobe damage in particular. The person is presented with sorting cards with a number of dimensions and colour concepts and shape but they are not told what the concepts are and they have to work it out as they go along. This is also a labouriously long test and they have to maintain concentration. A failure to maintain set is for example doing right 5 times and then inexplicably doing it wrong. Victims with frontal lobe damage may do that but most people with brain injuries don't do that. However 3 or more errors would be potentially suspicious unless there is a massive amount of frontal lobe damage.

Tests of Cognitive ability

1. **Test of pre-morbid functioning** – This is essentially a reading test for say, words like "debt". Except where the person is dyslexic this ought to be highly resistant to brain damage. It correlates highly with IQ tests and should be similarly matched. Reading ability should not be affected in cases of mild to moderate brain injury at least and this is regarded as a bench mark test.

2. **The Wechsler Adult Intelligence Scale IV test** – This is a test of brain injury and basic cognitive abilities. You can have good scores even with frontal lobe higher executive function deficits.

3. **Wechsler Memory Scales IV** – Flexible approach test- This is a recall test after half an hour's delay. A pattern of brain injury would mean that there is a big difference between the relative scores.

4. **The Conners' Continuous Performance Test -II** – This is a prolonged test. It is also lengthy. It is now usually administered by computer as are many of the tests. The person has to respond to every letter by pressing a key on the computer. It tests the ability to maintain concentration and not become distracted. Unlike most of the tests higher scores mean a worse performance. The higher the percentile, the worse the performance. People with ADD (Attention Deficit Disorder) normally have high scores on these tests.

5. **The DKEFS Verbal Fluency Test** – A test of verbal fluency. Deficiencies are often associated with damage to the left frontal cortex. Letter cues and animal cues are used to ask the participant to generate words.

6. **The D-KEFS Trail Marking Test** – This requires little cognitive ability and involves sequencing. It is fairly automatic and not a test of Executive function.

7. **The Wisconsin Card Sort Test** – Higher scores are better and mean better performance. This is particularly sensitive to frontal lobe damage;

8. **The Depression, Anxiety and Stress Scale** – These tests pick up on stress and irritability. The tests can help to pick up on changes due to brain injury.

Neuropsychologists also can help to treat and manage the effects of brain injury and are usually the ideal individual to treat the cognitive effects of cases of subtle traumatic brain injury.

Psychologist or neuropsychologist referral for treatment is often very helpful in the first instance to assist also in determining whether we are likely to be dealing with a case of pure psychological injury or whether there is also organic brain injury.

When attending for medico-legal appointments it is really important to ensure that:-

1. The Neuropsychologist has been well chosen. You may wish to consult with specialist counsel before choosing your experts;

2. Is well briefed and instructed preferably with the witness evidence and any treating notes in advance;

3. Testing is not being conducted within at least 6 months of any previous testing (due to memory of the previous tests and therefore the risk of invalid results);

4. The Claimant is well rested and arrives in good time with a good support structure in place;

5. Plenty of time is allowed for the appointment;

6. The Claimant is told of the importance of trying their best on the tests. The neuropsychologist will be able to tell if they are not trying their best and it may do their claim some harm if they do not.

Summary

- Neuropsychologists are specialist psychologists who treat and manage brain injury and are also able to identify particular areas of the brain which are underperforming through written batteries of tests.

- The tests are kept secret and are not published or sold outside the profession;

- There are tests of validity designed to measure unusual underperformance on the tests not consistent with brain injury. There may be other reasons for underperformance however other than deliberate underperformance;

- It is important that testing is not carried out at least within 6 months of each other.

- Repeat testing may be a useful measure of recovery or implementation of alternative strategies.

- It is very important that the Claimant is as well rested as possible. Overnight stays should be considered before hand if the Claimant has to travel any distance. An enhanced level of comfort of travel may be appropriate.

- Neuropsychologists are extremely highly trained and it can take over 7 years to train as a neuropsychologist. They are not medical doctors and are not psychiatrists however. The purpose of the report is not to conclusively diagnose brain injury and the severity of it but to perform and report upon a series of tests to help the Court and other experts.

CHAPTER TEN
MALINGERING

This has to be suspected when there is a failure of effort on the tests. The DSM IV criteria advised that malingering should be strongly suspected if any of the following are present:-

- Medico-legal context
- Discrepancy between complaints and objective findings
- Lack of co-operation
- Anti-social personality disorder

Does the history make sense?

- Is there any objective evidence of a head injury?
- Is the post traumatic amnesia or Retrograde amnesia unusual?
- Does the history differ from the records?
- Has the history changed over time or with different examiners or is a consistent history elicited?
- Has a mild TBI produced apparently severe deficits?
- Are there inconsistent results on tests measuring the same thing?

- Does test performance vary greatly from one occasion to another?

- Does performance become worse over time instead of better?

- Are the Claimant's emotions consistent with the reported gravity of the injury?

- Does the Claimant fail tests that they should pass e.g. effort?

Failed effort however is common in 42% of mild traumatic brain injury cases however and is not necessarily or always a sign of malingering. It may be due to psychological problems interfering with the testing.

What next, once you have a diagnosis?

We have to consider what we are seeking to achieve for the client. General damages, of course, but care and case management, aids equipment and loss of earnings are likely to be central to the claim in a case of subtle traumatic brain injury. We need to consider rehabilitation and consider an interim payment. The latter is not likely to be easy or straightforward in a Subtle, Traumatic Brain Injury case especially where the Defendant disputes causation and the diagnosis.

- Care and support issues- are likely to involve the need for personal care, help in dealing with and compensating for memory problems, disorganisation, motivation, disinhibition, anti-social behaviour and the Claimant's safety sometimes. We need to ask

  - Is the care necessary?
  - How much time is being spent?
  - Who should provide it for the future?
  - What hourly rate is appropriate?
  - Usually, a specialist brain injury care report will be obtained.

- Loss of earnings issues- are likely to involve projecting the career but for the accident and assessing the post-accident capacity for work. We want to know whether a structured return to work is possible and how this is going to be monitored? Is it appropriate for an Ogden 7 disability based future loss of earnings claim failing which, a Smith v Manchester type award? Some brain injured claimant's claims will relate to a failing business as their Executive Function may be diminished. Others will be able to work but will have failed at promotion or are so fatigued they can only work part time or they may feel that they cannot sustain it. It may take an actual medical recommendation to cause them to slow down and take more time off for rest and rehabilitation.

- Problems returning to work involve difficulties in organising, fatigue, epilepsy or the possibility of it and disinhibition and over-confidence sometimes blatant rudeness. I have had cases where the problems are not recognised until the Claimant tries to return to work and then the problems really become apparent. Appraisals and the personnel file are an extremely useful tool to analyse any problems. Statements from work colleagues or even customers are also essential.

Expert evidence and investigations

What does all this mean for the Personal Injury Practitioner?

Firstly, it means that for Claimant's lawyers they must listen to the Claimant and their family and not necessarily dismiss what they say in terms of cognitive difficulties and personality change which persist following the accident.

Defendant insurers and lawyers should be wary of the possibility of brain injury which may be initially missed but then later become apparent adding substantial alleged value to the claim later on.

Secondly, we must be cautious about accepting standardised orthopaedic opinions which make passing reference to head injury but diminish the injury or do not deal with it at all. It is the duty of an expert under Part 35 of the Civil Procedure Rules to set out where an area falls outside his or her Expertise and to say what further evidence is required to resolve the proceedings.

Claimant's lawyers should undoubtedly arrange a conference with the claimant and not just by telephone. In person, preferably or using video software at least. It is very important to see the visual expressions of the Claimant to see where and when they struggle.

As a Defendant lawyer you may need to warn about an increased reserve and look to early settlement. Be aware though that if a Claimant subsequently is said to have lacked capacity, a settlement has the potential to be avoided.

Thirdly, lawyers should be prepared to question the Orthopaedic Surgeon or General Practitioner about the possibility of a brain injury where the signs are present or indeed the lack of any signs. Claimant lawyers will need to prepare the ground for obtaining further reports.

Fourthly, Claimant lawyers should seek timely interim payments for the Claimant for treatment and rehabilitation where possible and referral to a Brain Injury rehabilitation programme such as that organised by the Oliver Zangwill Institute in Cambridge or seek a treatment regime, usually neuropsychological assessment and treatment organised with the assistance of a case manager appointed by the Insurers or independently by the Claimant.

An experienced Brain Injury Case Manager is almost certainly going to be of considerable assistance and the British Association of Brain Injury Case Managers can provide assistance as to whom to instruct in a given area. See http://www.babicm.org for more information.

Fifthly, if you are a Defendant you will almost certainly want to obtain covert surveillance of a Claimant who contends that their injuries are either escalating or where such injuries are not resolving and are alleged to be incapacitating. It's hard to detect brain injury by way of covert surveillance but evidence of normality and going out and about may be helpful if there is an allegation of malingering. What can sometimes be extremely helpful is not just visual surveillance but audio as well. Evidence of a Claimant with alleged injury or even incapacity performing a lengthy complex transaction with no evidence of hesitancy or fatigue or difficulty can be used with considerably devastating effect.

If you are acting for a Claimant you should expect such surveillance. The lack of objective outwards signs and the somewhat variable nature of minor traumatic brain injury may make it a target for sophisticated malingerers. The signs to watch out for which make malingering an issue are:-

- Very minor injury;
- Lack of any complaint in the medical context or at least until Litigation has started;
- Early suggestion by the Claimant or family that he is brain injured. Genuine claimants and their families often don't raise it themselves or suggest it;
- Serial Claimants;
- Failure of effort upon neuropsychological testing;
- Anti-social personality or convictions for dishonesty.

CHAPTER ELEVEN
SURVEILLANCE EVIDENCE

We have seen in the last chapter that malingering as a differential diagnosis cannot be ignored in any case and certainly not in Subtle Traumatic Brain Injury claims.

The capacity for malingering arises due to the compensation process and of course because of the lack of objective signs or evidence for the existence of brain injury. If the Claimant has a severe spinal cord injury or un-united severe leg fracture they can be imaged. The same for a severe or focal brain injury usually. With a more subtle brain injury, imaging as we have seen may not be a reliable indicator particularly where the injury is diffuse rather than focal.

The biochemical cellular disruption in brain injury often causes psychological problems and it is often not that helpful to distinguish between organic injury and psychological injury. Normally there is such considerable overlap between the two. The process can be influenced by mood and non-organic factors.

Part of the problem however is that Claimant's lawyers need to be sufficiently careful to elicit from their clients, the good days and the bad days. Even organic brain injury has some variability to it dependent on the stress upon the person day to day, how well rested they are and other non-organic factors including sub-conscious secondary gain.

The tendency to portray the worst case scenario must be avoided at all costs. The condition must be documented accurately and carefully and preferably contemporaneously.

In short, surveillance should be expected and the insurer's expectations managed. In this way, it should be manifestly obvious at an early stage to weed out the (hopefully) few claimants who are truly malingering or consciously exaggerating.

One of the problems with Surveillance in this area is that the Claimant is "walking wounded". Often there will be no outwards signs of disability or injury. Indeed, even upon casual acquaintance a person may not detect that the person is suffering from a STBI.

However, evidence of the ability to lead a normal busy life without fatigue, evidence of sociability, drinking, laughing and joking with friends, the ability to deal with complex transactions without apparent difficulty, working when the Claimant has said they don't or cannot, or evidence of deceitful behaviour in other ways perhaps towards a partner or spouse may be evidence of a high level of planning and ability which is inconsistent with the claimed brain injury. This can be quite properly devastating to a malingering claimant's case.

The recent decision of the High Court of Justice in Hayden v Maidstone & Tunbridge Wells NHS Trust [2016] EWHC (Q.B.) 1121 provided a thorough analysis of the law relating to surveillance. These key points arise:-

1. Video surveillance is a document for the purposes of the civil procedure rules;

2. It is privileged and need not be disclosed in part 1 of the standard disclosure form;

3. Where video evidence is available which the Defendant asserts undermines the case of the Claimant to an extent that it would substantially reduce the award of damages it will usually be in the overall interests of justice to require the Defendant to cross examine the Claimant and her medical experts upon it so long as this does not amount to a trial by ambush.

4. An ambush usually means in this context a deliberate delay in disclosure so as to achieve surprise. The Claimant must have a fair opportunity to deal with it.

5. A Defendant is entitled to wait until a Claimant has pinned his sail to the mast of a particular level of disability or collection of symptoms whether by a witness statement and/or a schedule of loss containing a statement of truth.

6. The Court will also have regard to when the Defendant ought reasonably to have commissioned such evidence. That must be when the Claimant's case in relation to the disabilities relied upon and their consequences is clearly articulated and the Defendant is in possession of an opinion from one of their medical experts that the claim is suspect.

7. Courts should more frequently consider the making of an order at the CMC for the "date by which" surveillance evidence should be disclosed if it is to be relied upon to avoid arguments about ambush.

In STBI cases both Claimants and Defendants lawyers and the insurers should be open to the *possibility* of malingering.

Witness statements need to be taken frequently and carefully as the litigation progresses by the fee earner responsible for the case and/or counsel.

If you are using Specialist, Counsel, instruct them early to assist in taking the witness statement from the Claimant often at the first meeting. It is so important to capture the statement in the Claimant's own words. It is so important to distinguish between what the Claimant remembers and what they have been told or reconstructed.

Open, non-leading questions and a detailed knowledge of the medical notes and history are essential.

Specialist Counsel should also know what the medical experts will be looking for, that is establishing in an accurate way, the levels of pre and post-traumatic amnesia. This can only be achieved by good cross referencing of the medical notes and open, non-leading questions of the Claimant.

The earlier it is done in the aftermath of the accident, the better as otherwise lapse of time is likely to interfere with the memory of the brain injured claimant in any event and render any witness statement potentially less accurate, or at least open to the charge of it being less accurate.

A diary kept by the Claimant or his or her partner can also be useful in compiling that witness evidence.

Mobile telephone bills may be useful to show the excessive reliance on others. It is surprising how mobile phone bills can tell the story. Some subtle brain injury claimants are forever phoning and sending SMS messages to their partner or family for information reminding them what they are supposed to be doing next and helping them structure their day.

Summary

- The witness statement is an important piece of evidence which should be taken carefully and early using open-non leading questions. Notes should be carefully cross-referenced;
- Diaries kept by the Claimant and their partner or family members will often assist. Mobile telephone bills may also demonstrate reliance on others.
- Surveillance can help to show malingering, contrary to popular belief that it is valueless in brain injury cases. Specialist Counsel should be able to help the Defendant determine what the surveillance operatives will be looking for.

CHAPTER TWELVE
DAMAGES

Firstly, in relation to General Damages for a claim in this class of brain injury claims, the Judicial College Guidelines 13th Edition (at present) will need to be considered. A specialist chapter in relation to "Brain and Head Injury" can be found at Chapter 3 of the Guidelines. The award should reflect the nature and severity of the symptoms rather than any diagnostic label according to the guidelines.

The likely categories of awards for STBI are:

- Category 3(c) (i) (ii) and (iii) "Moderate Brain Damage", £32,275–£183,150
- Category 3(d) "Less Severe Brain Damage", £11,650–£35,970
- Category 3(e) "Minor Brain or Head Injury", £1,675–£10,670

This is the full range of awards with the lower end not including a 10% uplift and the upper range including a 10% uplift. Readers should refer to the JC Guidelines themselves.

At the upper end there will be moderate to severe intellectual deficit, personality change, an effect on sight, speech and senses with a significant risk of epilepsy and no prospect of employment.

General Damages aside, it is usually the loss of earnings/profits claim which will be the second most important factor in a STBI case. For this reason, the highest value claims tend to be in respect of young professionals who have a clearly mapped career structure which they will be unable to achieve with the brain injury.

It is also important to consider a Disability claim under the Equality Act 2010 where the brain injury is likely to constitute a disability.

Briefly, a person is disabled if:-

1. They have an illness or disability which has lasted or is expected to last for over a year or it is a progressive illness;

2. They satisfy the Equality Act 2010 definition that the impact of the disability substantially (this means more than in merely a "trivial way") limits the person's ability to carry out normal day to day activities; **and**

3. Their condition affects either the kind **or** the amount of paid work they can do.

Normal day to day activities are those which are carried out by most people on a daily basis.

In relation to brain injury the following factors may in particular constitute disability. Precise reference should be made to the Act and the Guidance notes issues by the Secretary of State:-

Speech: Inability to communicate orally clearly with others or taking significantly longer to say things

Hearing: not being able to hear without the use of a hearing aid or the inability to understand speech under normal conditions.

Memory or ability to concentrate, learn or understand: for example intermittent loss of consciousness or confused behaviour or inability to remember names of family or friends. An inability to write a cheque without assistance or an inability to follow a recipe.

Perception of risk of physical danger: for example reckless behaviour, putting oneself or others at risk, This does not mean under-estimating the risk of dangerous hobbies.

Other likely claims are for the cost of ongoing specialist medication, the cost of a brain injury rehabilitation programme for help and assistance in organising daily lives, for a case manager perhaps but simply a "buddy" or "mentor" or "support worker" who can assist with memory and organisation and structuring the day.

Electronic aids such as electronic diaries, iPad, etc can also be proper heads of claim. STBI cases are potentially high value cases with the capacity to attract damages well in excess of £250,000.

Due to the potential for differential opinion and differing causes of the brain injury versus psychological effect and the potential for allegations of malingering it is not uncommon for there to be a very wide differential between the Claimant's pleaded claim and the admitted value of the claim by the Defendant. There is no doubt that such claims are fraught with risk for both parties.

CHAPTER THIRTEEN
PRACTICAL ADVICE

It is important when acting for a claimant to identify potential brain injury cases at an early stage and to obtain the appropriate evidence. Many are sadly missed and cases under-settled. If there is evidence of the signs of brain injury the first action should be to have a conference with the Claimant where a careful history of the signs and symptoms can be elicited and cross referenced with the full set of GP and hospital notes and ambulance notes.

You may then wish to ask the orthopaedic or A &E expert or GP about the potential for a brain injury if the signs and facts fit the potential for such a disorder and ask them to make recommendations for further evidence.

It would be usual to obtain evidence from a Neurologist . You may decide that a Neuropsychological referral is appropriate straight away and then perhaps a Neuro-radiologist and then to obtain your Neurolo - gical report. No two cases of brain injury affect the Claimant in exactly the same way.

You will need to cross refer reports to the other experts and this will need to be budgeted.

Defendants may wish to tactically offer interim payments for treatment even where causation is uncertain. It may be cheaper in the long run even if such costs are not always recovered where the claimant fails in relation to causation. The Insurer should also abide by the industry agreed "Serious Injury Code" which was updated in September 2016.

They will almost certainly in any case which is "suspicious" want to perform frequent surveillance on the Claimant and to obtain their own medical evidence normally from a Neurologist and Neuro-psychologist and Neuro-psychiatrist.

If acting for a Claimant, lawyers will wish to ensure that frequent witness statements are taken from the claimant as the litigation progresses and if possible that a diary and care schedule are maintained by the claimant.

The use of medical experts and Counsel who have specialist knowledge of this type of brain injury can save costs in the long run and improve the outcome of the litigation especially if involved from the earliest stage where the condition is suspected or where symptoms have not resolved within prognosis.

CHAPTER FOURTEEN
A CASE EXAMPLE: SIEGEL V PUMMEL

There is one relatively recent case which is probably essential reading for anybody engaged in this area as it illustrates many of the issues which arise in this area. This is the case of Peter Asher Siegel v Lester Pummell [2014] EWHC 4309.

This case was heard at trial by Mr Justice Wilkie in the High Court of Justice in London and Judgment given on 18th December 2014. The full judgment extends to 91 pages.

Proceedings arose out of a seemingly relatively minor road traffic accident which occurred on 16th November 2009. Liability for the accident was admitted. The Defendant's car struck the Claimant's car whilst the Claimant was stationary at traffic lights in Norwich. The estimated speed of the collision was between 20 and 35 mph.

After the accident he complained of visual disturbances and a severe headache. There was no appreciable or documented loss of consciousness after the accident. Crucially however, he did remember hitting his head against the head restraint. He also remembered leaning to the left prior to the accident to change the radio station. He then did not remember getting out of the car. He could not recall speaking to the other driver for 10 to 15 minutes nor describing his Daimler as his pride and joy nor being angry with the Defendant and telling him that he was uninjured. He could not recall the days following the accident or if he went into the office in the days following the accident. He now knows he sent some emails but was unaware whether that was in the hotel or the office.

After he returned to work in January 2010 things did not improve much. He said he had become short tempered, had lost his organisational skills and lateral thinking required to put the project back on track. He felt he was eventually forced out of his job and resigned. He also said he had lost his ability to multi-task, lacked social judgment and would suddenly blurt out inappropriate comments. He suffered mental fatigue and had less empathy to others.

As the Judge put it, the parties were "fundamentally at odds" in relation to the issue of quantum. The claim was put forwards by the Claimant in the sum of £2,172,235 of which £75,000 was by way of General Damages for Pain, suffering and Loss of Amenity.

The Defendant's counter-schedule denied that any damages arise save in respect of general damages for which the Defendant said the Claimant stood to be compensated for the sum only of £5,000.

The Claimant's claim arose from a cluster of cognitive, physical and behavioural deficits that he attributed to a severe subtle, permanent closed brain injury attributable to Diffuse Axonal Injury.

The Defendant's position was that assuming the Claimant's reported symptoms were genuine, the Claimant had not suffered any brain injury but had suffered psychological upset and a mild whiplash injury. The psychological upsets were always going to occur in his life said the Defendant. The Defendant also said that his problems were likely to be iaterogenic, subconsciously arising from the expectations of his medical and legal advisers who erroneously informed him that he had sustained a brain injury in the accident.

The Claimant had been a high achieving person with an outstanding academic background who went onto become an IT systems designer and engineer.

The Claimant's neurologist was of the view that loss of consciousness was a poor guide to the presence of brain injury. The trial was hard fought and a plethora of medical and psychological experts and witnesses were heard on both sides.

The judgment is one well worth reading in full.

In short, the Judge found that:-

1. Mr Siegel's symptoms were caused by Diffuse Axonal Injury of the brain. The Judge rejected the Defendant's contention that in the absence of evidence of loss of consciousness, a normal GCS score and an absence of lesions a DAI is conclusively ruled out.

2. Psychological causes were ruled out as not being the probable cause although the Judge did not rule that psychological symptoms in an appropriate case may cause similar symptoms.

3. The Judge accepted that iaterogenesis is also one potential cause for such symptoms although this was not the case here.

4. The Judge awarded £65,000 General Damages and other damages amounting to a total of almost £1.6 million.

The key features which ensured success for the Claimant in this case were that a detailed, careful forensic approach was taken by the Claimant's legal team right from the outset. Medical and other experts were chosen with care and the witnesses and statements taken were highly persuasive. Key literature was used in support of the arguments that DAI can occur without profound loss of consciousness. The marker of Post traumatic amnesia was identified and carefully used as an indicator of and the severity of the brain injury. In short, the case contains many useful pointers for the practitioner whether acting for the Claimant or the Defendant.

There is little doubt that this niche area of Personal Injury Law is probably in its infancy and set to grow. It has very great implications for Claimants, the insurance industry and possibly also in relation to the engineering and design of motor vehicles as well.

ABOUT THE AUTHOR

Pankaj attended Leeds Grammar School and Magdalene College, Cambridge. He was called to the Bar in 1997. He undertook pupillage at Zenith Chambers, Leeds and is now a practising Barrister and full tenant at both 12 King's Bench Walk, London (since 2008) and Exchange Chambers, Leeds, Manchester, Liverpool (since 2012).

Pankaj grew up within a medical family and is fast becoming a recognised leading name with specialist expertise in brain injury cases. He represents both Claimants and Defendants usually only in high value life-changing and catastrophic injury cases. He has an excellent understanding of medical issues. He has addressed an international conference held at the Royal Society of Medicine.

Renowned for his meticulous eye for detail and sensitive client approach, he is described as having "*wide-ranging expertise' including 'brain injuries, chronic pain and psychiatric injuries*" (The Legal 500, 2015). In 2016 the Legal 500 found that he is "*recognised for his expertise in brain injury cases*".

Pankaj is routinely instructed nationally by leading firms. He is sought after by insurers too and adopts a team approach with the insurer and Solicitor. He is a Deputy District Judge and has considerable expertise in costs management of high value cases for both Claimants and Defendants.

He is experienced in claims of the utmost severity exceeding £5 million.

Pankaj enjoys keeping fit, photography, travel, the theatre and the opera. He is from a medical family background and is married to a Consultant Child Psychiatrist and is a dad to a 6 year old.

MORE BOOKS BY LAW BRIEF PUBLISHING

'A Practical Guide to Holiday Sickness Claims' by Andrew Mckie & Ian Skeate
'Ellis and Kevan on Credit Hire, 5th Edition' by Aidan Ellis & Tim Kevan
'RTA Allegations of Fraud in a Post-Jackson Era: The Handbook, 2nd Edition' by Andrew Mckie
'RTA Personal Injury Claims: A Practical Guide Post-Jackson' by Andrew Mckie
'A Practical Guide to Personal Injuries in Sport' by Adam Walker & Patricia Leonard
'A Practical Approach to Clinical Negligence Post-Jackson' by Geoffrey Simpson-Scott
'A Practical Guide to Costs in Personal Injury Cases' by Matthew Hoe
'Occupiers, Highways and Defective Premises Claims: A Practical Guide Post-Jackson' by Andrew Mckie
'Employers' Liability Claims: A Practical Guide Post-Jackson' by Andrew Mckie
'Baby Steps: A Guide to Maternity Leave and Maternity Pay' by Leah Waller
'The Queen's Counsel Lawyer's Omnibus: 20 Years of Cartoons from the Times 1993-2013' by Alex Steuart Williams

These books and more are available to order online direct from the publisher at www.pibulj.com, where you can also read free sample chapters. For any queries, contact us on mail@lawbriefpublishing.com or telephone 0844 587 3283.

Our books are also usually in stock at www.amazon.co.uk with free next day delivery for Prime members, and at good legal bookshops such as Hammicks and Wildy & Sons.

We are regularly launching new books in our series of practical day-to-day practitioners' guides. Join our free newsletter to be kept informed: www.lawbriefpublishing.com

www.ingramcontent.com/pod-product-compliance
Ingram Content Group UK Ltd.
Pitfield, Milton Keynes, MK11 3LW, UK
UKHW020150290926
15471UKWH00004B/793